Old Fort Niagara

An Illustrated History

by
Frederic Ray

LA SALLE AT THE SITE OF FORT NIAGARA — In December, 1678, the great French explorer, Rene Robert Cavelier, Sieur de La Salle, sailing across Lake Ontario from Fort Frontenac, landed on the barren point of land where Fort Niagara now stands. With La Salle were his famed lieutenant, Tonty of the Iron Hand, and the missionary priest, Father Louis Hennepin. A small fort was constructed at this point commanding the mouth of the Niagara River. This was the first Fort Niagara; La Salle called it Fort Conty. Exploring up the river, Father Hennepin discovered the mighty cataract of Niagara Falls. Permission to build a vessel on the river above the falls was granted to La Salle by the Seneca Indians who dominated the region, and construction was begun on the "Griffon." The following August she left Squaw Island, the first vessel to sail the upper Great Lakes. La Salle moved on, leaving a small garrison at Fort Conty which was soon afterwards destroyed by fire and abandoned.

THE MILLET CROSS — It was nine years before a French expedition on campaign against the Iroquois and commanded by the Marquis de Denonville, governor of New France, landed at the site of La Salle's first fort (July, 1687). Here the marquis built "a fort of pales, with four bastions" which he called Fort Denonville. He left 100 men at this small post under Chevalier de la Troye. A terrible winter of bitter cold, starvation and disease was the fate of this small band of Frenchmen, beset by wolves and surrounded by unfriendly Indians from whom they could expect no succor. A rescue expedition reached the fort on Good Friday, 1688, and found only 12 men left alive! One member of the rescue party, a Jesuit, Father Millet, erected an 18-foot cross within the fort before which he said a mass invoking God's mercy for the stricken garrison. The following September Fort Denonville was abandoned.

The present Millet Cross, a replica of the original, bearing the abbreviations, "Regn. Vinc. Imp. Chrs." was declared a National Monument by President Calvin Coolidge in 1925.

THE LEGEND OF THE HAUNTED WELL — A duel between two French officers in the Castle of Fort Niagara provides us with the legend of the haunted well. Fighting for the favor of a local Indian maid, the encounter culminated in the death of one of the officers in the vestibule. The victor cut off his rival's head, threw the body down the well and tossed the head into Lake Ontario. The well was sealed up by the English at a later date and was only recently discovered through the original plans of the fort found in Paris. According to the legend, the ghost of Fort Niagara still haunts the Castle at midnight in search of his head.

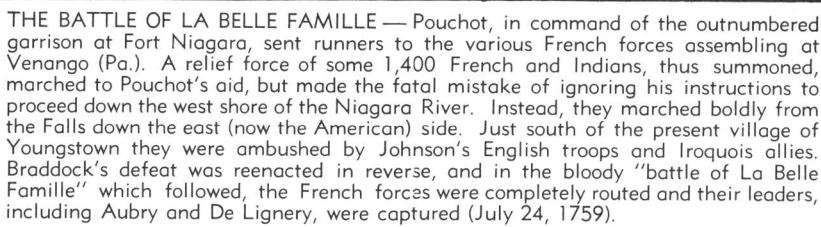

THE BATTLE OF LA BELLE FAMILLE — Pouchot, in command of the outnumbered garrison at Fort Niagara, sent runners to the various French forces assembling at Venango (Pa.). A relief force of some 1,400 French and Indians, thus summoned, marched to Pouchot's aid, but made the fatal mistake of ignoring his instructions to proceed down the west shore of the Niagara River. Instead, they marched boldly from the Falls down the east (now the American) side. Just south of the present village of Youngstown they were ambushed by Johnson's English troops and Iroquois allies. Braddock's defeat was reenacted in reverse, and in the bloody "battle of La Belle Famille" which followed, the French forces were completely routed and their leaders, including Aubry and De Lignery, were captured (July 24, 1759).

In his dispatch to Amherst, Johnson wrote, "The action Begun about half after nine; But they were so well Received by the Troops in front & the Indians on their Flank that in an Hours time the whole was Compleatly Ruind & all their Officers made Prisoners. . . . I cannot ascertain the Number of the Killd, they are so dispersd among the Woods, But their Loss is Great. . . ."

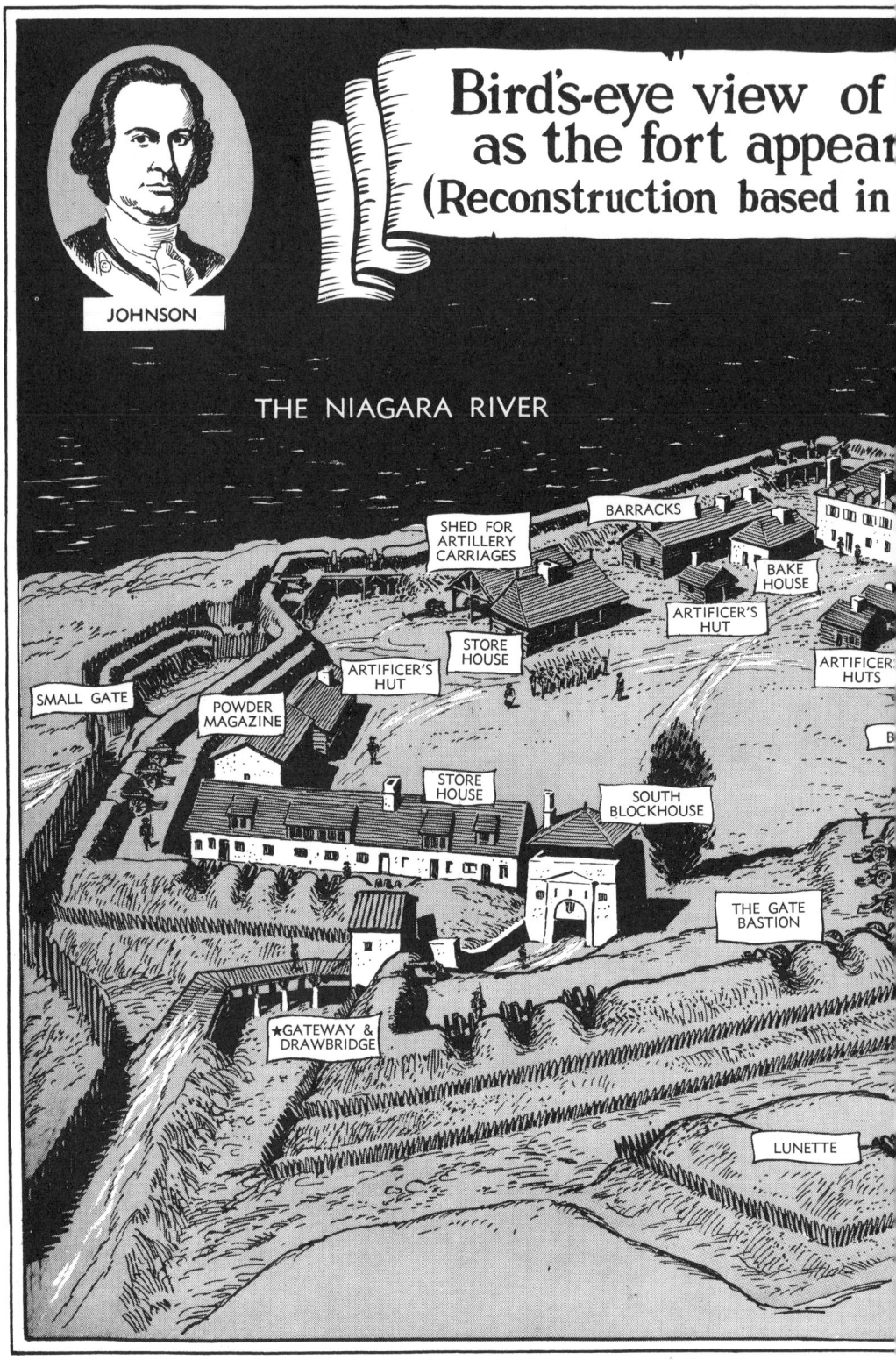

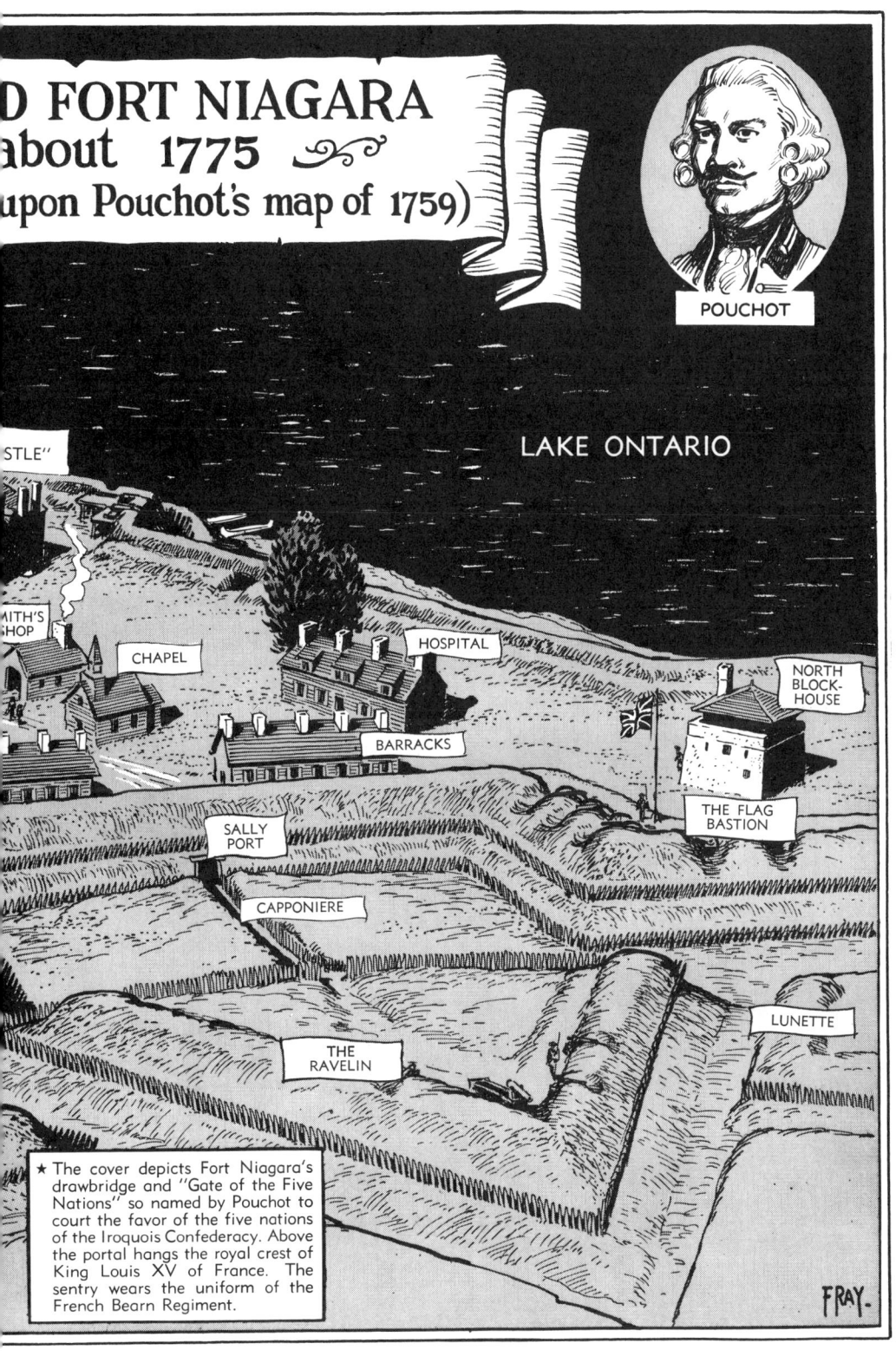

THE FRENCH SURRENDER FORT NIAGARA — Pouchot was incredulous when he heard that his relief force had been defeated. He sent an officer under a flag of truce to the British lines to see first hand the prisoners taken in the battle. Thus convinced, and with all hope of assistance gone, Pouchot surrendered the fort on July 25, 1759, Johnson restraining his savage Iroquois from falling upon the French column as it left the fort. The siege had lasted 18 days, and the ramparts of the fort, especially the Flag Bastion, had suffered heavily from British mortar fire. With the fall of the key post of Niagara, the remaining French positions in the west became untenable and the upper lakes and Ohio valley were opened to English control. Two months later Quebec fell to the British and France ceased to be a power in the New World.

Sir William Johnson, first British commandant of Fort Niagara, had been appointed by the crown to be superintendent of all North American Indians, and in this capacity he wielded great influence over a vast frontier territory.

The blockhouses at Old Fort Niagara were built by the British in 1770-71. These redoubts were so designed that the roof could be completely dismantled on short notice to prevent danger of flying splinters in case of a direct hit by enemy artillery. The buildings accommodated 20 soldiers. The north redoubt is here shown.

FORT NIAGARA DURING THE REVOLUTION — During the American Revolution Fort Niagara was a British base of warfare against the American colonists on the frontier. It was the seat of Col. John Butler's Tory Rangers, who, assisted by Iroquois warriors under Chief Joseph Brant (Thayendanegea), carried out the bloody raids on the settlements in Cherry Valley (N.Y.) and Wyoming (Pa.). Back to Niagara came these marauding parties with American scalps and prisoners. So serious became the threat to the American frontier that General Washington, in 1779, sent General John Sullivan and an army against the Iroquois. Sullivan drove deep into hostile country, destroying villages and crops and reaching the Genesee River, 84 miles from Fort Niagara, before turning back because of lack of supplies.

Although the war ended in 1783, Fort Niagara was not officially relinquished to the United States until 1796. During this "holdover" period thousands of Tories, or "Empire Loyalists," fleeing from the states to Canada, passed through the portals of Old Fort Niagara.

THE BATTLE OF QUEENSTON HEIGHTS — With the outbreak of the War of 1812, General Van Rensselaer, commander at Fort Niagara, undertook the capture of Queenston Heights, across the Niagara River (October 13, 1812). The American attacking force succeeded in taking a bluff overlooking the village of Queenston. While rallying his men, British General Isaac Brock was killed. The Americans, abandoned in the attack by the New York militia, who refused on technical grounds to cross the river and invade enemy territory, were finally overwhelmed and taken prisoner. The captives included Colonel (later Lt. Gen.) Winfield Scott, who had distinguished himself during the engagement. After his exchange by the British, Scott became adjutant at Fort Niagara under General Dearborn, and later led an American army to victory over the British at the battle of Chippewa in 1814; he was wounded at Lundy's Lane a few days later.

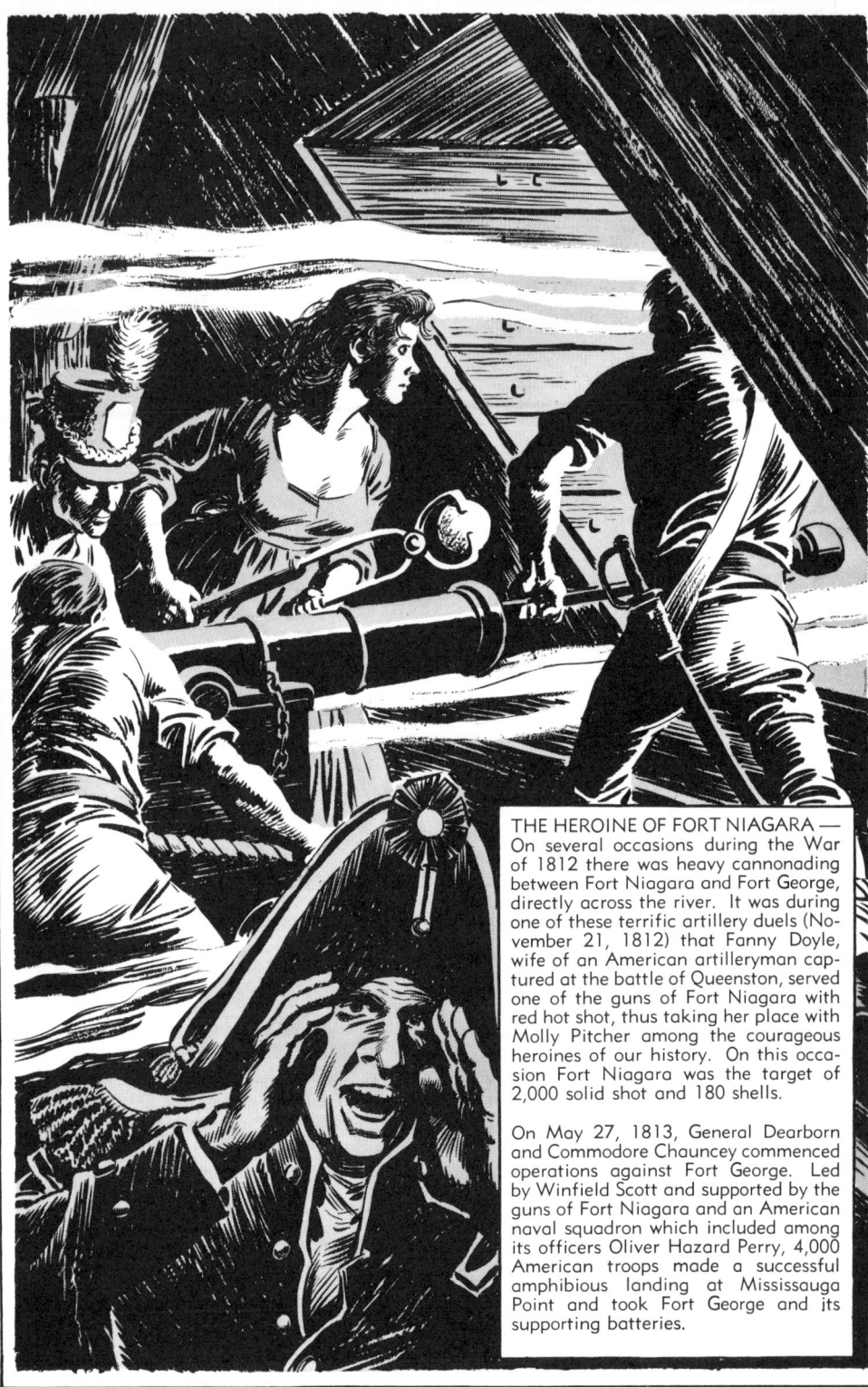

THE HEROINE OF FORT NIAGARA — On several occasions during the War of 1812 there was heavy cannonading between Fort Niagara and Fort George, directly across the river. It was during one of these terrific artillery duels (November 21, 1812) that Fanny Doyle, wife of an American artilleryman captured at the battle of Queenston, served one of the guns of Fort Niagara with red hot shot, thus taking her place with Molly Pitcher among the courageous heroines of our history. On this occasion Fort Niagara was the target of 2,000 solid shot and 180 shells.

On May 27, 1813, General Dearborn and Commodore Chauncey commenced operations against Fort George. Led by Winfield Scott and supported by the guns of Fort Niagara and an American naval squadron which included among its officers Oliver Hazard Perry, 4,000 American troops made a successful amphibious landing at Mississauga Point and took Fort George and its supporting batteries.

THE BRITISH CAPTURE FORT NIAGARA — In December, 1813, General McClure, in command of American forces holding Fort George, heard that British regulars and Indians were moving against him. He thereupon burned the village of Newark, spiked the guns of Fort George, which the British soon reoccupied, and retreated to the American side of the river. On the night of December 19th, 1,000 British and Indians, thirsting to avenge the burning of Newark, quietly crossed the river several miles upstream and stealthily advanced on Fort Niagara. In a surprise assault they easily gained entrance to the fort (the drawbridge gate was found open!) and there followed a wholesale bayoneting of the small garrison, most of whom were scarcely awake. The American loss was 80 killed, 14 wounded, and 244 made prisoners. Within a few days the entire Niagara Frontier, from the fort to, and including, Buffalo was a heap of smoking ruins. In 1815, with the conclusion of peace, Fort Niagara was again restored to the United States.

LATER YEARS — The year 1817 witnessed the signing of one of the most noteworthy of international agreements, the Rush-Bagot Treaty between England and the United States. This treaty limited the naval armament on the Great Lakes and was the forerunner of the later feeling of mutual trust and friendship which has resulted in the complete disarmament of the Canadian-American border of nearly 4,000 miles, the second longest international boundary in the world. The treaty is commemorated by a memorial erected north of the Castle along the lake shore.

During the Civil War the defenses of Fort Niagara were strengthened in anticipation of possible British intervention in behalf of the South. It was during this period that the brick casemates of the fort were constructed (pictured here).

Today Old Fort Niagara affords the visitor a fascinating and authentic window into the past, with its earthworks, drawbridge, five pre-Revolutionary stone buildings, forty-nine mounted cannon, and a hot-shot furnace (believed the only one in northern United States). The fort, at Youngstown, N. Y., is operated by the Old Fort Niagara Association, a non-profit organization, under license from the Niagara Frontier State Park Commission, and is open to visitors daily the year round.